Come on, Tim

Story by Jenny Giles
Illustrated by Judith Love

Tim looked at the fort.

He saw Michael and Anna playing on it. They climbed up the ladder and came down the pole.

Tim went to the fort.
He saw Michael and Anna
climbing up.

Tim climbed up, too.
He climbed up
to the top of the fort.

Michael went down the pole.
Then Anna went down.
She went down **fast**.

"I will go down the pole, too,"
said Tim.
"I can do it."

Tim looked down.
He saw the children playing and he saw Mrs. Hill.
He saw Michael and Anna coming up again.

"Go on, Tim," said Michael.
"Go down the pole."

"Go on, Tim," said Anna.

"You go first," said Tim.

Mrs. Hill went to the pole.
She looked up at Tim.
"Come on down," she said.
"I will stay here by the pole."

"Come on, Tim!" said the children.
"Come on! Come on!"

Mrs. Hill said,
"I am here, Tim. You can do it."

Tim got on to the pole.
He looked down at Mrs. Hill.
"Here I come," said Tim,
and he went slowly
down
the
pole.

"I did it!"
shouted Tim.
"I went
down the pole."

"You **did** it,
Tim,"
said Michael.